RELOCATING GOD'S VERSION OF ME

Robert Fitzgerald

Relocating God's Version of Me

Trilogy Christian Publishers

A Wholly Owned Subsidiary of Trinity Broadcasting Network

2442 Michelle Drive

Tustin, CA 92780

Copyright © 2024 by Robert Fitzgerald

Scripture quotations marked NIV are taken from the New International Version. Copyright © 1973, 1978, 1984, 2011 by Biblica, Inc®. Used by permission. All rights reserved worldwide.

Scripture quotations marked NKJV are taken from the New King James Version®. Copyright © 1990 by Thomas Nelson. Used by permission. All rights reserved.

Scripture quotations marked KJV are taken from the King James Version®. Public domain.

Scripture quotations marked AMP are taken from the Amplified Bible. Copyright © 2015 by the Lockman Foundation. Used by permission.

All rights reserved, including the right to reproduce this book or portions thereof in any form whatsoever.

For information, address Trilogy Christian Publishing

Rights Department, 2442 Michelle Drive, Tustin, CA 92780.

Trilogy Christian Publishing/ TBN and colophon are trademarks of Trinity Broadcasting Network.

For information about special discounts for bulk purchases, please contact Trilogy Christian Publishing.

Trilogy Disclaimer: The views and content expressed in this book are those of the author and may not necessarily reflect the views and doctrine of Trilogy Christian Publishing or the Trinity Broadcasting Network.

10 9 8 7 6 5 4 3 2 1

Library of Congress Cataloging-in-Publication Data is available.

ISBN 979-8-89333-123-3

ISBN 979-8-89333-124-0 (ebook)

DEDICATION

This book is dedicated to my Lord and Savior Jesus Christ, my wife Rochelle, and my children.

"Then the LORD God called to Adam and said to him, 'Where are you?'"

(Genesis 3:9, NKJV)

CONTENTS

INTRODUCTION..9

CHAPTER 1: PREDATION...16

CHAPTER 2: COMPETITION..24

CHAPTER 3: COMMENSALISM.......................................34

CHAPTER 4: INTERLUDE —
  A MESSAGE FOR THE BRIDE OF CHRIST...............40

CHAPTER 5: PARASITISM..50

CHAPTER 6: MUTUALISM...62

CHAPTER 7: WHY THIS MATTERS.................................72

INTRODUCTION

Have you ever found yourself making a decision in which you may have gained something yet lost yourself in the process? Let's look at this in practical terms. You accepted that job offer yet its schedule and demands have negatively impacted your closeness to God and your family. You jumped into that relationship yet lost your purity and God's purpose for your life. You made that huge purchase, yet you took on such a great debt that you can't financially plan for the things God wants to prepare you for.

Some of you may feel discouraged and hopeless, thinking, I made this decision and now I can never relocate God's plan for my life. But that's a lie. This book was inspired by a series of teachings the Lord gave me to present to the young adults small group I led at my home church on Tuesday nights. Not only am I writing about it, but I have gone through this season myself. Because God is bringing me through it, I wanted to encourage you with this truth: you can relocate God's version of you if you are willing to go on this journey.

There's a wonderful invention called the GPS. According to Aerospace.org, GPS stands for "Global Positioning System." The US piggybacked off Russia's launching of Sputnik, the first satellite to successfully orbit the earth in 1957. Through research, the US discovered that the closer Sputnik was to their location, radio frequencies increased; the further away, those signals decreased. Nasa.gov tells us that in the 1960s, the US went on further to test this hypothesis by launching additional satellites to detect some of their submarines carrying nuclear missiles. The satellites detected the submarines' radio signals within a few minutes, making the experiment a success.[i]

Today, GPS has different uses with different levels of access. We civilians use it to locate vacation spots and to track our Uber Eats driver. However, there is a level of access that we civilians do not have that our government has. It's called PPS, or the Precise Positioning System. I see God saying to us today, "If you would partner with Me on this journey of relocating My version of you, you don't have to be limited to this civilian-level access where you see things in the natural and make decisions based on carnal, earthly reasoning. If you return to relationship with Me, then I'll do in your life what it says in Proverbs 3:5–6 (NKJV), 'Trust in the LORD with all your heart, and lean not on your own understanding; in all your ways acknowledge Him, and He shall direct your paths.'"

You won't have to depend on your favorite YouTuber or social media influencer for advice because they are operating on a civilian level. There are threats on larger scales that you need to be able to detect, so you need access to God's GPS. Threats to your God-given identity, threats to your children, your marriage, your family. Threats to the things God has prepared for you. If you don't relocate God's version of you, you won't know who you really are in the battle. You'll think that you're a civilian when God has called you to be a general. One of the greatest threats to the enemy is you truly locating who you are in Christ, because once you find who you are, you will find your God-aligned purpose—which, in turn, destroys the enemy's purpose for your life.

How many of you have used a GPS before, but even though you arrived at the address, you still couldn't identify the exact building or house? In those times, I usually call the person at the place I'm trying to find. In turn, they give me a specific description so that I'm able to know exactly where to go. Similarly, it is impossible for us to locate the God-version of me if I don't have a description of what that is. What is the God-version of me? I will begin by starting in the book of Genesis.

According to Genesis 1:26–28 (NKJV),

> *God said, "Let Us make man in Our image, according to Our likeness; let them have dominion over the fish of the sea, over the birds of the air, and over the cattle, over all the earth and over every creeping thing that creeps on the earth." So God created man in His own image; in the image of God He created him; male and female He created them. Then God blessed them, and God said to them, "Be fruitful and multiply; fill the earth and subdue it; have dominion over the fish of the sea, over the birds of the air, and over every living thing that moves on the earth."*

When I study the Word of God, I love to dive into the deeper meaning. I examine details such as the original language, culture, customs of the time, and even the sociopolitical context. My young adults know that I'm a self-proclaimed word nerd! In the first part of that portion of Scripture, God decided to create mankind in His image. "Image" in Hebrew is *"tselem,"* which means "something cut out."[ii] We are cut out from God Himself—in other words, we are pieces of God. Because we are cut out from God, we have the DNA of God in us! Think about all of your different characteristics. The creative side of you comes from God. Your ability to empathize with another's feelings comes from God. The side of you that exercises judgment, reason, and common sense comes from God. Your ability to love passionately comes from God. Now these characteristics were tainted by the fall of man, but we'll get into that later.

Next, God chose to create us according to His likeness. "Likeness" in Hebrew is "*demuth*," which refers to being like God.[iii] Notice that we are not God, but we are like God. Because we are created in His likeness, our words, thoughts, and actions should be a reflection of who God is.

God then gave mankind dominion over all living things on earth. The Hebrew word for dominion is "*radah*," which means "to have dominion, rule, dominate."[iv] Let's be clear: This is not the world's concept of ruling like some narcissistic dictator—God's way is different, and we will also discuss this later in the series. Your ability to rule and dominate is connected to the God-version of yourself. Some of us are wondering why things might not be working out in different areas of our lives. It may seem like we aren't making an impact in our industry, and we might be frustrated. In these instances, we must ask ourselves two things: (1) Have I located the God-version of me that has His authority to rule? (2) Do I have the legal, God-given authority to rule in the environment where I'm frustrated?

First, have we located the God-version of me that has His authority to rule? Let me preface this question with the fact that there is a season of preparation. Some of these issues are a matter of time and patience. David did not become king overnight—he went through a process that involved testing, suffering, patience, and submission to God. Jesus went through His own season of testing on earth before He became our risen Savior and King. The difference between them and many of us is that Jesus and David already located the God-version of themselves. Their issue was a matter of patient endurance. The Word of God tells us that through faith and patience, we inherit God's promises for our lives (see Hebrews 6:12). Unlike David and Christ, some of us are delusional, expecting to walk in God's authority without even starting the journey of locating the person He has called us to be.

Second, we must consider the environment we are in. We must ask ourselves, "Do I have the legal, God-given authority to rule in the environment where I'm frustrated?" Sometimes, it's not just a matter of locating the God-version of ourselves, but we also need to understand that to successfully rule, we must know the domain—or territory—in which we have been given the divine, legal authority to rule. A king's authority is only as valid as the territory over which he has the legal authority to rule. I'm not prophesying, but if the president of Russia tried to come to the US and establish his government in the White House, then there would be some serious problems. Why? Because our current president went through the process that gave him the legal authority to be president of the United States of America. That's why I get really nervous when I hear about the idea of setting up colonies on Mars because according to Genesis, man's divine authority to rule has been designated to earth.

Let's sum it up. If you don't relocate God's version of you, you won't be able to tap into the authority that He has designated for you. If you don't discern the territory over which God has designated you to rule, you will find yourselves in conflict with the authority God has placed over you. You will neglect or totally miss out on the place God has destined for you to move in His authority.

I'm a special education teacher, and two years ago I had the awesome privilege of co-teaching biology. As I started writing this series, the Holy Spirit reminded me about the five types of relationships between organisms. Initially, one would ask, "What does this have to do with relocating God's version of me?" Then Holy Spirit brought this truth to me: "Losing the God-version of yourself has mainly to do with who or what we disconnected from and who or what we connected to."

In this book, we will examine the five biological relationships through the lens of God's Word and discuss how they apply in our lives. Through this teaching, God will help us to discern how the things or persons we are connected to might be impacting our ability to locate God's version of us.

The images at the beginning of each chapter give further insight into the topic examined. You will also notice that each chapter ends with a prayer along with discussion questions. Feel free to utilize these resources during your personal devotional time. If you lead a small group, consider incorporating this book into a seven-part series. In each meeting, you can accompany a chapter and its discussion questions with other planned activities.

Relocating God's version of ourselves is a process. But the first step we need to take is a willingness to admit that we may not have located God's version of ourselves yet. After Adam and Eve disobeyed God and ate the forbidden fruit, they hid from Him. Genesis 3:8–10 says, "And they heard the sound of the LORD God walking in the garden in the cool of the day, and Adam and his wife hid themselves from the presence of the LORD God among the trees of the garden. Then the LORD God called to Adam and said to him, 'Where are you?' So he said, 'I heard Your voice in the garden, and I was afraid because I was naked; and I hid myself.'"

God is omniscient—all knowing—so it's not like He didn't know where Adam and Eve were. God asked Adam this question because He wanted Adam to be honest about the fact that he had lost God's version of himself. We start this journey by asking God a few honest questions:

God, where am I right now?

Am I truly living Your version of life for me, or am I living some counterfeit version of myself that will ultimately lead to destruction?

I might even know You, yet have I settled for a lesser version of myself right now?

INTRODUCTION: DISCUSSION QUESTIONS

1. How did mankind's loss of their God-intended identity originate in the garden of Eden?

2. Why is our spiritual enemy—Satan—threatened by individuals who discover their God-given identity?

3. What could be at stake in our lives if we do not locate God's version of ourselves?

4. What is the first step to relocating God's version of ourselves? Why is this first step absolutely necessary?

5. Why is locating God's version of ourselves a process rather than instantaneous? What factors can make the process longer or shorter?

6. In the introduction, I likened finding one's God-given identity to our nation's use of GPS, as well as our military's use of PPS. How do the differences between both systems relate to us spiritually?

7. According to the Holy Spirit, what does relocating God's version have to do with relationships?

Chapter 1

PREDATION

Earlier I mentioned a key truth that the Holy Spirit revealed to me. He said to me, "The losing of oneself has mainly to do with who or what we disconnected from and who or what we connected to." When you are connected to something or someone, you have established a relationship with that person or thing. It is important to discern the nature of that relationship. Many of us have lost the God-version of ourselves because we have not discerned the nature of the different relationships we are in. As I said before, God reminded me of the five types of relationships between organisms in biology. They are predation, competition, commensalism, parasitism, and mutualism. Today, we are going to examine predation.

In predation, one organism eats another organism to obtain nutrients. In this type of relationship, only one party benefits: the predator or the stronger organism. In the image at the beginning of this chapter, a mountain lion—the predator—is chasing a deer. The prey completely loses out on everything because the prey is weaker and, in most cases, even smaller. Our enemy, the devil, is a vicious predator. John 10:10 refers to him as the thief who comes to steal, kill, and destroy. There is a reason why Jesus listed these verbs in this order because each successive verb is more severe than the previous one.

First, the devil comes to steal. He starts the process of theft through his lies, just as he lied to Adam and Eve in the garden of Eden. You may think that the first thing Satan stole was Adam and Eve's innocence and ability to live. No, the first thing he stole was their attention. God had spoken clearly to Adam and Eve about what they could and could not do. The moment Eve gave her ears to the serpent's words and her eyes to what he had to offer, destruction's time bomb started ticking.

Today, there are many things competing for our attention. Why do you think companies spend so much money on advertisements? According to statista.com, in 2021, businesses in the United States spent a total of $297.5 billion on advertisements alone.[v] Businesses know how valuable your attention is to them. If they get your attention, they will eventually get your money. As I write, many of us are being robbed right now due to what we are giving our attention to (you may even be distracted by your cellphone now as you're reading this!). Pastor Touré Roberts had some wise words concerning this. I remember him saying, "Whenever you give attention to something, always ask yourself, 'What is this thing taking my attention from?'"

In Adam and Eve's case, when they gave their attention to Satan's words and the fruit he offered, this temptation took their attention from God and God's words. Things went downhill because Adam and Eve went from hearing and seeing to touching and tasting. I hear God telling us today that immediately stopping Satan at the ear and eye gate of our hearts will prevent us from going down a path that will lead us further away from God's purpose and, ultimately, into destruction.

Let's make it practical. The moment you notice that a TV show or commercial is heading in the wrong direction, change the channel or even shut off the TV. Change the playlist. End the conversation and walk away if you need to. Some may think, *Well, that's rude*, but that decision could save your life.

Next, the devil comes to kill. The Greek word for "kill" is "*thyo*," which means "to slaughter."[vi] Let's be clear, this is not a simple bullet to the head. Think about animals in a slaughterhouse. They are completely dismembered. The devil wants to completely slaughter the person God originally designed for you to be. Think about what is happening in our society today. Think about what the enemy is trying to do to children and young people today. Gender-changing pills and medical procedures are literally slaughtering the God-given gender and sexuality of many in our society today. Consider the mass shootings that have taken place in our country. Many of the shooters were lonely, confused, and wounded individuals whom the enemy lied to. Because they gave their attention to his lies, they allowed

Satan to turn them into vicious monsters who ended the lives of many—in most cases, even their own. Some of their victims were even children.

Finally, the devil comes to destroy. The Greek word for "destroy" is "*apollumi*," which means "to kill or render useless."[vii] As a kid, my family and I would sometimes watch those nature TV shows. When a pack of lions pounce on their prey, they don't just neatly eat the meat and leave the bones, but they completely destroy the carcass until it is virtually unrecognizable. This is what the enemy wants to do to us.

Many who have had their gender changed by medical procedures can no longer physically go back to the man or woman God originally intended for them to be. Yes, they can still give their hearts to the Lord and return to being their gender to a certain extent, but, unless God does a creative miracle by regrowing their reproductive organs, their bodies are forever mutilated. Satan wants to do worse than even this. He wants to destroy us to the degree that we will no longer feel useful to God and His kingdom. Why do so many of us sin and then feel guilty, ashamed, and even suicidal? The devil knows that, if we continue to nurse those emotions, we won't return to God and His version of ourselves who will serve God effectively. Fortunately, Jesus Christ took on our guilt and shame and died on the cross for us so that we can return to God and the version of ourselves He intended us to be.

The question we must ask ourselves is, "Am I in a prey/predator relationship with someone or something?" Usually, prey/predator relationships are pretty overt—it's obviously destructive because the bondage or attack is in your face. This type of relationship can take on many different forms. It can be a substance that you find yourself addicted to, which will ultimately destroy your health and cut your life short. It can be pornography or sexual addiction which threatens to destroy your marriage and your concept of sex or sexuality. It could be an abusive relationship that is endangering your physical well-being and causing you to feel worthless. It could be a destructive habit. Maybe you are used to lying, cheating, or manipulating your way through situations. Those habits will lead to destruction. The unifying characteristic of any prey/predator relationship is the obvious fact that something or someone connected to you has the potential of completely destroying you.

Please listen carefully: If we do not relocate God's version of ourselves, we will be easy prey for the enemy. When we are God's version, we are victorious over the enemy. Romans 8:37 (NKJV) says, "We are more than conquerors through Him who loved us [referring to Christ]." Returning to the God-version of yourself means that you, now, find your identity in Jesus Christ; therefore, you are no longer under the power of your old, sinful nature. Second Corinthians 5:17 (KJV) tells us, "Therefore if any man be in Christ, he is a new creature: old things are passed away; behold, all things are become new."

I don't know about you, but staying in the counterfeit version of myself is not an option. I can't just sit back passively while a substance addiction is robbing me of finances, breaking my family apart, and destroying my health. I need to get back to the God-version of myself. I can't just sit back and allow pornography to destroy my marriage and potentially fall into the hands of my children—now creating a generational curse of sexual addiction. I must get back to the God-version of myself. If I am unmarried, I can't stay in that relationship that is toxic and harmful to me and my physical well-being (if you are married and in an abusive relationship, please remove yourself from danger and connect to resources that will provide a safer, healthier alternative. National Domestic Violence Hotline: 800-799-7233). I need to get out of that relationship and relocate God's version of me. I've got to get rid of that old version of myself that lied, cheated, and manipulated to survive because the Bible tells me that liars and thieves will not inherit the kingdom of heaven (1 Corinthians 6:10). I must relocate the God-version of myself.

To wrap things up, are you in a prey/predator relationship with someone or something? The Holy Spirit has a simple two-word command for you: "Get out!" Ask Him for the wisdom and courage to leave.

Please pray with me: *Father in the name of Jesus, I acknowledge that there could be a predator in my life threatening my well-being (pause for a moment and quietly ask the Lord to show you who or what that predator is). Father, I ask for You to give me the will and strength to separate myself from (if alone, name the predator) because it/he/she has the potential to completely destroy the person You intended for me to be. As I move along this journey with You, please heal me of every wound and help me to relocate Your version of me. In Jesus's name, amen.*

CHAPTER 1: DISCUSSION QUESTIONS

1. Why is one's attention of great importance to the enemy? Why should this make us cautious?

2. Why is it crucial that we immediately flee temptation upon its initial presentation? What are some practical ways in which we can do this?

3. In John 10:10 (NIV), Jesus said, "The thief comes only to steal and kill and destroy; I have come that they may have life, and have it to the full." Explain the severity behind the words "steal," "kill," and "destroy."

4. How does Jesus Christ offer hope to those who feel as though their identity has been totally destroyed?

5. How is a predatorial relationship easy to detect?

6. Why is remaining a counterfeit version of ourselves not an option?

7. What is the Holy Spirit's simple command for those in a prey/predator relationship? How can they apply this command to their lives?

Chapter 2

COMPETITION

In the previous chapter, we discussed the first of five biological relationships, which is predation. We read from John 10:10, which reminds us that our enemy—the predator—comes to steal, kill, and destroy. We looked at those words in their original language and realized that each verb is progressively worse than the other. The devil wants to steal our attention away from God, violently slaughter us, and destroy our lives. But the rest of John 10:10 encourages us. Jesus stated, "I have come that they [referring to us] may have life, and have life to the fullest, or more abundantly" (paraphrase). We ended by asking God to reveal to us anything or anyone who is a predator in our lives and prayed for the courage to separate ourselves from that person or thing. We also asked Him to heal us and to restore us to the God-version of ourselves.

The second biological relationship we are going to examine is competition. In biological terms, competition is when organisms compete for the same resources. Because there are not enough resources to sustain both organisms, only one organism comes out surviving. Competition can lead to the extinction of certain species. Biologyonline.com tells us that hyenas and adult male lions in Kenya compete for the same prey.[viii] If one predator is consuming the prey at a rate disproportionately higher than the other, it can lead to the other predator's extinction.

How does this relate to us? There are some relationships that are rooted in unhealthy competition. I'm not talking about the type of competition in which both parties care about each other and are friends at the end of the day. I am referring to a type of competition fueled by greed, jealousy, and ego. I'm talking about the type of competition leading to strife, division, backstabbing, sabotage, character assassination—even the type that could result in greater offenses. If we find ourselves demonstrating these negative fruits toward others to get what we want, then did God provide what we obtained?

Remember that the fruit will always match its seed. In other words, watermelons will always come from watermelon seeds. Grapefruit will always come from grapefruit seeds. When we sow the fruits of the Spirit—love, joy, peace, patience, gentleness, goodness, and faith (Galatians 5:22–23)—we can be confident that what we reap comes straight from God. However, if you had to backstab, cheat, or make someone look bad to get what you want, then your fruit did not come from God—no matter how good it might look to others. Remember that, on judgment day, God is not going to reward our works based on how appealing they were to others; He will reward us according to the motives behind what we did (Jeremiah 17:10; 1 Corinthians 3:13–15).

It's interesting because a few verses prior to the fruit of the Spirit, Paul tells us, "For you, brethren, have been called to liberty; only do not use liberty as an opportunity for the flesh, but through love serve one another. For all the law is fulfilled in one word, even in this: 'You shall love your neighbor as yourself.' But if you bite and devour one another, beware lest you be consumed by one another" (Galatians 5:13–15, NKJV). Essentially, Paul is saying that jealousy-fueled competitive relationships clash with God's purpose of adding souls to His kingdom. Think about it. A person tired of the dog-eat-dog, every-man-for-himself nature of the world may come into the house of God seeking a healthier and more nurturing environment. However, if that man sees the same—or in some cases, worse—behavior, it is very likely that he may not return. He will probably share his negative experience with others, and they will avoid going to the house of God as well. The end result of this is a languishing church. If you are a believer in Christ, please listen carefully: toxic competitive relationships are stripping many Christians of their main purpose of demonstrating Christ's love and truth to the world. We are losing our God-given identity by engaging in these types of relationships, and this problem must be taken seriously.

Think about King Saul in 1 Samuel. He was anointed as the first king of Israel. God made him some amazing promises—contingent on Saul's obedience to Him. As we know, Saul was disobedient twice. First, he did not wait until Samuel arrived at Gilgal to offer his sacrifice but offered it too early out of fear that his armies would scatter from him. Second, he did not completely destroy the Amalekites as the Lord commanded him to do (1 Samuel 10:8; 13:8–14; 1 Samuel 15). As a result, the Lord told Saul that He would strip the kingdom of Israel from Saul and give it to another. David was the person God would give the kingdom to.

Without going into every detail of the story, David was a shepherd-boy-turned-giant-slayer whom Saul noticed, and he essentially hired David to become his armor bearer. However, in 1 Samuel 18:1–9, things shifted quickly after both David and Saul returned from the battle against the Philistines. The women sang, "David slayed his ten thousands and Saul his thousands" (v. 7, paraphrase). Upon hearing this, Saul viewed David as his competition rather than God's way of blessing him and Israel.

If you are a leader in any capacity, whether in ministry or the secular field, please listen. God could send someone your way to be a blessing to you, but you can block yourself from the blessing if you perceive that person as a threat. For example, the pastor of a struggling church could be reaching out to God for help. In answer to that pastor's prayer, a person gifted in the areas of need arrives. That man or woman's assignment is to bless you, encourage you, and to help build your ministry. If you are not careful, you might think that they are in competition with you even though this isn't their intention at all. (Note: This is not to say that every person who walks into your ministry will have the right intentions. As a leader, you will need to have spiritual discernment and act accordingly if the person has been assigned by the enemy to sow discord or rebellion. As Christ told us in Matthew 7:16 (NKJV), "You will know them by their fruits.")

Without hesitation, allow God to deal with any jealousy or insecurity you may have in your heart. Left unchecked, these sinful emotions can lead you to attack the very person sent from God—resulting in a missed blessing and even worse: God's judgment. Remember, the Word of God warns us, "Do not touch My anointed ones, and do My prophets no harm" (Psalm 105:15, NKJV).

Yes, Saul lost the kingdom through disobedience. But think about it: He didn't have to lose his relationship with God. If he humbled himself enough to accept losing a temporary throne, then he would not have seen David as a threat because God had already blessed Saul in different ways. He was described as good-looking, had a wife and children, and still had some time to enjoy being king. One of the effects of envy-fueled rivalry is that our focus on our perceived rival blinds us to the blessings God has right in front of us. Attempting to match or supersede them, we end up losing God's version of ourselves.

I want to make this very applicable today. Let me preface this by saying that some of these words will cut deep but only so that we can allow God to address these areas of our heart lovingly yet firmly. Some of us are blinded by our friends on social media. We get so caught up in the clothes they're wearing, their current vacation, or the person they are in a relationship with. As a result, we lose appreciation for our spouses, family, and other blessings from God—in some cases even neglecting them. We find ourselves living superficial lives emulating those friends rather than Christ Himself. Some of us become so filled with jealousy that we can't even stand to see those people on social media any longer. We begin to harbor hatred in our hearts for these people, not realizing that God equates this to murder (Matthew 5:21–22). We find ourselves making backhanded comments undercutting our friends' successes. We are no longer the persons Christ originally intended for us to be.

Tragically, we see this in Saul's story. He quickly lost the God-version of himself and never relocated it. He went on to be tormented by an evil spirit, committed attempted murder against David several times, consulted a witch before going into battle, and eventually killed himself. Even after Saul's death, David's heart broke for him—reflecting the very heart of God for Saul (the Bible says that David was a man after God's heart in 1 Samuel 13:14). Today, God's heart is breaking for those of us caught up in unhealthy competition. He is calling us to repent and to return to Him, our First Love.

Some of us may be on the other side of competition. In our love for Christ, we are using our gifts to glorify Him, edify the body of Christ, and to bring positive change within our industry. However, we may have unwillingly developed enemies of our success along the way and find ourselves—like David—constantly dodging their attacks. I have a word of encouragement for you. You don't have to feed into their behavior. Stay humble. Pray for those individuals. Don't take matters into your own hands because God said in His Word, "Vengeance is mine; I will repay" (Romans 12:19, KJV). Many of us have heard this saying before: Winning isn't everything. This is true! Earthly achievements will come and go. In the grand scope of eternity, our spiritual condition is most important.

Abraham, known as the father of faith and a friend of God, is a great example on how to handle a relationship with an unhealthy sense of competition. In Genesis 12, God told Abraham (then Abram) to leave the idolatrous city of Ur, located in the Chaldean Empire. God promised to make Abram's name great and to multiply his offspring into a great nation. The command to leave and the promise of greatness was for Abram; however, Abram decided to allow his nephew Lot to tag along with him. As both men traveled together, they individually increased in household size, livestock, and possessions but realized that there weren't enough resources or space in their current location of Bethel for both of them to remain together. Initially, this resulted in great strife between both parties. But in Genesis 13:8–9 (NIV), Abram came to a wise conclusion and told Lot, "Let's not have any quarreling between you and me, or between your herders and mine, for we are close relatives. Is not the whole land before you? Let's part company. If you go to the left, I'll go to the right; if you go to the right, I'll go to the left."

Abram had enough confidence in God's promises to refrain from unhealthy competition. This is the key to victory over these types of relationships! Think about it: If we have to manipulate, cheat, or step on others to acquire the resources we need, then is God truly our source? I'm not saying that we will not struggle at times, but we won't need to mimic the dog-eat-dog culture to meet our needs. You see, the God-version of you knows that God will supply all of your needs according to His riches and glory (Philippians 4:19). The God-version of you knows that if you seek first the kingdom of God and His righteousness, then everything you need will be added to you (Matthew 6:33).

Let's make it practical. The God-version of you knows that, in your singleness, you don't need to hate or throw shade on others just to get noticed, because you're trusting God to find your spouse. The God-version of you knows that you don't need to take someone else down in order to get a position, because God is the one who raises up one and puts down another (Psalm 75:7), and if you humble yourself in the sight of the Lord, He will exalt you in due season (1 Peter 5:6). The God-version of you knows that the cross will lead to a crown—therefore, you do not need to bow your knee or sell your soul to the devil to step into authority because the Word of God tells you that if you suffer with Christ, then you will reign with Him (Romans 8:17). The God-version of you doesn't need to use carnal weapons to bring change on the earth or in our nation because the Word of God says, "If my people, who are called by my name, will humble themselves and pray and seek my face and turn from their wicked ways, then I will hear from heaven, and I will forgive their sin and will heal their land" (2 Chronicles 7:14).

Whatever side of a competitive relationship you find yourself on, relocate your God-version by humbling yourself and returning to Him in heartfelt repentance. Stop seeing others as your rival, because our heavenly Father created you both uniquely for His purposes while cherishing you the same. Value and nurture the blessings that God has given you rather than envying others' blessings. If you are the target of one's envy, don't seek vengeance; rather, pray for the person, use godly wisdom around them, and trust the Lord to fight your battles.

For those with an unhealthy sense of competition, please pray with me: *Father, I repent of ungodly rivalry. Forgive me for allowing covetousness, jealousy, and my own insecurities to control my behavior toward others. Please cleanse my heart and replace those negative characteristics with Your humility and love. In Jesus's name, amen.*

If you find yourself the target, please pray with me: *Father, I forgive those who have hurt me due to their own jealousy. Please change their hearts. Help me to continually trust You to fight my battles, and may I never repay evil with evil. In Jesus's name, amen.*

CHAPTER 2: DISCUSSION QUESTIONS

1. Describe the differences between healthy and unhealthy competition.

2. Why should a person fueled by unhealthy competition reevaluate the source of his or her blessings?

3. Explain how unhealthy competition results in a dying church. Consider Galatians 5:15 as you answer this question.

4. Describe the ways that an unhealthy sense of competition can blind us.

5. How did Saul get caught up in unhealthy competition? What lessons should leaders learn from Saul's life?

6. How did Abraham respond differently from Saul when faced with unhealthy competition?

7. What is the key to victory over unhealthy competitive relationships?

8. How should we respond if we are the target of someone fueled by envy?

Chapter 3

COMMENSALISM

In Latin, commensalism means "to eat at the same table."[ix] In biology, it is a "unique relationship between two species wherein one species draws food, shelter, or transport from the other without harming it."[x] The species providing the food and shelter is the host; the one benefiting from the host is the commensalist guest. The image at the beginning of this chapter shows a bird, called the cattle egret, perched on top of a wildebeest. While the wildebeest grazes, insects cleave to their body. The egret benefits from the wildebeest by eating insects off its body—neither benefiting nor harming the wildebeest. A second example is a spider building its web between shrubs. The spider benefits because she has support for her web, but the shrubs are neither positively nor negatively affected. The gist is that only the guest benefits in commensalism. The host neither benefits nor is harmed.

In nature, this type of relationship is no cause for alarm. However, in terms of our spiritual journey, the parallel is a great cause for concern. Many have fallen into a delusion in which they consider their actions inconsequential. Have you ever heard someone say, "I can keep doing this as long as it isn't hurting anyone"? Take a smoker for example. In their mind, this vice is their own business; one need not concern himself with the smoker's issue. We know that this is far from true as studies have proven that secondhand smoke inhalation is more dangerous than primary smoking.

Similarly, many have drifted into a detached, indifferent mindset about where they stand with God. They believe in God and even acknowledge His role as Creator and the One who controls everything. However, these individuals do not consider that their words, thoughts, or actions impact Him—nor do they allow God to impact the way they live. It is a type of deist belief system. For those who don't know, deism is the belief in the reality of God and His role as Creator; yet deists consider God to be uninvolved in man's affairs. The problem with this thought is that there is no need to feel conviction of sin, because if God is uninvolved in man's affairs, then man does not need to be accountable to God; man could just do his own thing.

Commensalism, in essence, describes neutrality in the way one impacts another. But the Word of God teaches us that, in Christ, there is no neutrality. In Matthew 12:30 (NIV), Jesus said, "Whoever is not with me is against me, and whoever does not gather with me scatters." In Revelation 3:14–16 (NIV), Jesus warned the church of Laodicea, "I know your deeds, that you are neither cold nor hot. I wish you were either one or the other! So, because you are lukewarm—neither hot nor cold—I am about to spit you out of my mouth." The truth is that commensalism does not exist in the kingdom of God. There is no neutral territory—no Switzerland, if you would—in the spiritual war we are in. Someone told me about a skit in which a man was sitting on a fence. On one side of the fence, Jesus beckoned the man to follow Him. On the other side of the fence, Satan called the man to him. The man, indecisive, determined that the fence was the most comfortable place for him to remain. However, Satan then says to the man, "Welcome to hell: I own the fence."

Such is the case of those who have developed a false sense of neutrality concerning light and darkness. Many of us have deceived ourselves into thinking that we can have this type of relationship with God and be fine. We can say the sinner's prayer, go to church on Sundays, but the rest of the week, we say to God, "You do You and I'll do me. I did the church thing on Sunday and I'm good. Now it's time for me to live my life my way for the rest of the week until I see You again on Sunday." You continue living in fornication (sex outside of marriage), engaging in illegal activities, mistreating others, harboring grudges and unforgiveness for the rest of the week. We treat God like an acquaintance. In reference to relocating God's version of ourselves, this state is most dangerous because of the self-deception of thinking that we are fine with God *when we are not*.

God does not have acquaintances. You either know Him or you don't know Him! We see this in what Jesus told a man in Luke 13:22–27 (NIV). It says,

> *Then Jesus went through the towns and villages, teaching as he made his way to Jerusalem. Someone asked him, "Lord, are only a few people going to be saved?" He said to them, "Make every effort to enter through the narrow door, because many, I tell you, will try to enter and will not be able to. Once the owner of the house gets up and closes the door, you will stand outside knocking and pleading, 'Sir, open the door for us.' But he will answer, 'I don't know you or where you come from.' Then you will say, 'We ate and drank with you, and you taught in our streets.' But he will reply, 'I don't know you or where you come from. Away from me, all you evildoers!'"*

The individuals that Jesus described in this portion of Scripture were comfortable with relegating Him to the role of a casual acquaintance. They said to Him, "We ate and drank with You ... You taught in our streets." It's interesting because it goes back to the Latin meaning of commensalism, which is "to eat at the same table."

Let me give it in terms that you can understand. There was a brief moment in my life in which I worked for an elected official. I experienced times in which I was only a few feet away from well-known politicians. You would recognize some of them on TV. I even shook hands with a few of them. Yet, I did not have a personal relationship with any of them. I did not know them intimately; neither did they know me intimately. I would have been delusional to think that I could just show up at their front door, ring their doorbell, and somehow, they would just let me in. On the contrary, they would call the cops on me—and rightfully so! Why do we think that it is any different with God? We need to have a personal relationship with Him. In fact, locating God's version of ourselves starts with us entering into a personal relationship with Him. In Revelation 3:19–20 (NIV), a few verses away from the Scripture we read about lukewarmness, Jesus said, "Those whom I love I rebuke and discipline. So be earnest and repent. Here I am! I stand at the door and knock. If anyone hears my voice and opens the door, I will come in and eat with that person, and they with me."

In summary, commensalism is a relationship in which neither party benefits nor harms the other; yet we know that this type of relationship can never exist between us and God. The reality is that we are either a friend of God or a stranger to Him, working for Him or working against Him. It is time for us to consider our ways.

If you have found yourself in a neutral zone, neither for nor against the Lord, please pray with me: *Father, I confess that I have been lukewarm and indifferent in my attitude toward You. I realize that it is time for me to choose this day whom I will serve, and I declare that it is You that I will serve. I repent of all evil associations and hypocritical behavior such as _____ (please be specific). Thank You for Your forgiveness. I welcome You into my heart and surrender to Your Lordship over my life. In Jesus's name, amen.*

CHAPTER 3: DISCUSSION QUESTIONS

1. Describe ways in which our personal choices could have a major impact on others.

2. Explain how commensalism is a form of deism.

3. Describe the moral problem presented when mankind considers God to be uninvolved in their affairs.

4. In terms of the spiritual battle we are in, explain why taking a neutral stance is dangerous.

5. Why is it delusional for a person to think that a casual acquaintanceship with Christ is acceptable?

6. According to Revelation 3:19–20, what hope does Jesus offer to those who are of the commensalist, lukewarm mindset?

7. What are some ways in which we can draw a line and eliminate a neutral mindset in our personal lives?

Chapter 4

INTERLUDE – A MESSAGE FOR THE BRIDE OF CHRIST

So far, we have covered the first three of our five biological relationships: predation, competition, and commensalism. By examining these relationships through the lens of God's Word under the Holy Spirit's guidance, we were able to understand how each represents the things or persons in our lives impacting our ability to relocate God's version of us.

After teaching these first three relationships to my young adults, I was preparing for my Bible study on the fourth relationship when I experienced a divine interruption. The Holy Spirit revealed some major things to me following a dream I had. Now we know that the ultimate source of revelation is the Word of God, but there are many examples within the Bible itself where God spoke to individuals through dreams and visions—ranging from Joseph in the Old Testament to John the apostle in the New Testament. Moreover, in Joel 2:28 (NIV), the Lord said about the last days, "And afterward, I will pour out my Spirit on all people. Your sons and daughters will prophesy, your old men will dream dreams, your young men will see visions." The ultimate litmus test for any dream or vision is, does it align with the Word of God? If it does not align, throw it out! Allow the Holy Spirit and God's Word to be your standard as you read what I am about to share. By the way, this is not some random chapter I decided to insert; you will soon see how it relates to relocating God's version of ourselves.

My dream was quite simple with a profound meaning. I dreamed that I was looking for my sandals in my dad's house in Queens, New York. I put on my sandals and left his house. When I woke up from the dream, God gave me Psalm 45:10–11 (NKJV), which says, "Listen, O daughter, consider and incline your ear; forget your own people also, and your father's house; so the King will greatly desire your beauty; because He is your Lord, worship Him."

Psalm 45:10–11 is describing a woman preparing for marriage. As a single woman, her father is her covering. For her to be married, she needs to leave her father's house in order to come under her new covering, her husband. This truth also applies to a man planning to marry a woman. We see this in Genesis 2:24 (NIV) when God first instituted marriage: "That is why a man leaves his father and mother and is united to his wife, and they become one flesh."

The Holy Spirit then led me to Genesis 31 which describes the intense conflict Jacob had with his father-in-law Laban. Jacob had reached his limit with Laban. For those who aren't familiar with the story, here is the summary: After returning to his family's region, Jacob fell in love with a woman named Rachel. Her father, Laban, promised to grant Jacob Rachel's hand in marriage if he committed to working for Laban for seven years. However, at the end of the seven years, Laban broke his promise and gave Jacob his older daughter, Leah, in marriage. He made Jacob work for another seven years in order to marry Rachel. In essence, Laban used his own daughters—Leah as a pawn and Rachel, a bargaining chip—to exact more work out of Jacob. Imagine how Leah and Rachel must have felt! Laban was a shrewd, deceitful man whose home was filled with idolatry. Despite Jacob's authority as the head of his wives and family, Laban wanted to remain in control. Jacob took his wives and other items from Laban's home, feeling justified because the Bible says that Laban cheated Jacob by changing Jacob's wages ten times (see Genesis 31:7).

As believers, we are like Leah and Rachel. The Word of God calls us the bride of Christ. In 2 Corinthians 11:2 (NIV), Paul stated, "I am jealous for you with a godly jealousy. I promised you to one husband, to Christ, so that I might present you as a pure virgin to him." Laban is a type of Satan, our former father. Due to Adam's sin, we became children of the enemy by default. This is why Jesus told those who did not believe in Him, "You belong to your father, the devil, and you want to carry out your father's desires" (John 8:44, NIV).

God told Jacob to leave Laban's house. Why? The reason is because God, the bridegroom, was preparing to establish His union with the nation of Israel—and, later on, with us! You see, God would later change Jacob's name to Israel. The entire nation of Israel, the Jewish people, descended from Jacob's twelve sons. Jesus Christ, the Savior of the world and every believer's bridegroom, descended from Judah, one of Jacob's twelve sons. What if Jacob's wives declined his invitation to leave with him and remained under their father's roof? They could have gotten comfortable there. After all, Laban was very wealthy and they were, in some ways, benefiting from him. Here is what might have happened if they remained: The destiny of an entire nation—and, potentially, of all mankind—could have been negatively impacted. We know that Laban was deceitful and unscrupulous. Based on his history with Jacob, Rachel, and Leah, there was no limit to the harm Laban could have inflicted. What if he decided to give Jacob's wives away to other idolatrous men in his community? Where would the nation of Israel be? Where would the rest of us be? The Holy Spirit unveiled a sobering truth to me through this story: *We cannot stay under the enemy's covering and be the bride of Christ at the same time.* Our decision to either stay or leave will not only impact our destinies; it will also affect the destinies of those connected to us. Just as Rachel and Leah had a choice to either leave Laban's house with their husband Jacob or remain there, we have a choice as well. God is not content with allowing His bride to continue living under Satan's bondage and oppression. God is the one who comes in power to take us, His bride, from under Satan's covering.

In Matthew 12:29 (NIV), Jesus said, "Or again, how can anyone enter a strong man's house and carry off his possessions unless he first ties up the strong man? Then he can plunder his house." We know that Christ is all-powerful, so the strong man—Satan—is no match for Him. In different parts of the gospels—Matthew through John—we see demons flee at one rebuke from Christ. Christ's strength is not the issue here. However, unlike inanimate items in a house, we have free will. When Christ comes into our lives to bring us out from under the enemy's covering, we have a choice to either stay within that ungodly, oppressive environment or to come out and allow Christ to be our new covering. It requires us to leave everything about our father's house that was unhealthy, ungodly, and contrary to God's Word, character, and nature. We are now a part of a covenant relationship with our bridegroom, Jesus Christ. Today, God firmly yet lovingly urges us to separate ourselves from the ungodliness in this world: "Therefore, 'Come out from them and be separate,' says the Lord. 'Touch no unclean thing, and I will receive you.' And, 'I will be a Father to you, and you will be my sons and daughters, says the Lord Almighty" (2 Corinthians 6:17–18, NIV).

Leaving Laban's home was the catalyst to Jacob finding God's version of himself. Had Jacob and his wives remained under Laban's roof, Jacob could have missed the powerful encounter he had with God in Genesis 32. In obedience to God's directive, Jacob and his wives were enroute to Jacob's homeland when one of Jacob's servants informed him that Jacob's older brother Esau was on his way with 400 men to meet Jacob. This was not good news for Jacob! Earlier in Genesis 25 and 27, we learned that Esau held a grudge against Jacob because Jacob stole Esau's birthright and firstborn blessing when they were younger. Now, in Genesis 32, before Esau arrives, Jacob has an encounter with God. Jacob wrestles with God all night and prevails! God changes Jacob's name from "deceiver and supplanter" to "Israel" which means "Prince of God." In biblical times, the meaning of an individual's name usually determined their character and even revealed their destiny.

Relocating God's version of ourselves means that we have a life-changing encounter with God that transforms our character and changes our destiny for the better! You see, not only did God change Jacob from being a lying manipulator, He shifted Jacob's destiny, making him the prince and leader of a great nation. Whatever your character flaws and current situation, God wants to encounter you! He wants to transform you into the best version of yourself that you could possibly be—His version! He wants to transform your destiny to the degree that you will leave a positive impact on future generations. Think about what is at stake: your family, children, descendants, city, nation. God may even want you to impact several nations!

We saw that God changed Jacob's name to Israel after their encounter. It's interesting because, when a woman marries a man, she usually drops the last name she inherited from her father and takes the last name of her husband. When we leave the enemy's kingdom and submit ourselves in love to Christ's lordship, we take on Christ's character and identity like a new last name. But for this to happen, we must first leave our old covering. Some women choose to take on their husband's new name but still include their father's last name with a hyphen. In rare cases, some women choose to altogether keep their father's name without taking the name of their husband. In the natural, this is okay, but not in the spiritual! When we are married to Christ, we are fully His and must carry His name only!

So, in the spiritual realm, what is your last name? In other words, whose identity do you bear? Is it that of your old father, the devil? Or is it the identity of Christ, the bridegroom? You who claim to be the bride of Christ, does the spiritual realm see you bearing His name? Do they see a combination of your old and new names—representing lukewarmness and compromise? Or do they see the old name only—you not demonstrating any evidence that you belong to Jesus Christ?

Shortly after teaching this portion of the series, the Holy Spirit asked me, "How far are you willing to go for love?" He is asking you this question today. You see, true love compels an individual to do whatever is necessary to be with the one he or she loves. Isn't that what Jesus Christ did for us? Consider this: He had it made in His heavenly abode. He was surrounded by glory, had all the heavenly host of angels at His command, and was in perfect harmony with the Father and the Holy Spirit. He saw us, His most-prized creation, in our sinful state; yet He still loved us. His love compelled Him to forsake what was comfortable, be born and live as a man, suffer, and die on the cross just so that we could be with Him forever. How insulting it must be to Christ that many, despite His sacrificial love, reject His offer to rescue them from the enemy's covering. Our old father, the devil, deceived them into thinking that it is better to remain under his rulership. As a result, they have settled for these conditions. In their false comfort, they have become blind to their current bondage and impending judgement. John described their condition perfectly: "This is the verdict: Light has come into the world, but people loved darkness instead of light because their deeds were evil" (John 3:19, NIV).

Beloved, true love demands a change! When one understands and receives the love of Christ, perceiving the depth of His sacrifice and the length He took to save us, that individual will leave his or her old life to follow Christ. This act is known as repentance. It is the message that John the Baptist preached in paving the way for Christ's earthly ministry. In Matthew 3:2 (KJV), John exhorted his Judean countrymen, "Repent ye: for the kingdom of heaven is at hand." According to Thayer's Greek lexicon, the word "repent" in its original Greek is "*metanoeó*," which means "to change one's mind for the better, heartily to amend with abhorrence of one's past sins."[xi] In other words, when we repent, we change our minds about the life we lived under Satan's dominion. We no longer consider it to be pleasurable, comfortable, socially acceptable, or even politically correct. We see our sin for what it truly is: hateful, destructive, detestable to God, and worthy of His judgement. We develop a genuine godly sorrow that pushes us beyond emotions into actions leading us out from our old lifestyle and into the life Christ offers us.

My friend, are you willing and ready to accept Christ's invitation to come out from your old, sinful covering to be His true bride? You may even call yourself a follower of Christ, yet your manner of thinking, speaking, and acting reveal that you are still abiding under Satan's covering. I know this will sound harsh, but please do not deceive yourself: you are not the bride of Christ. Remember, the true bride of Christ will leave her old covering behind to come under His covering. It is better for you to hear this now than when you stand before God's throne on the other side of eternity. It will be too late to change then. You have a choice today. Please do not let the enemy deceive you into thinking that you can make the decision tomorrow, for tomorrow is promised to no one. You must completely submit to Christ's covering. This act demands that you leave your old way of living, walk in obedience to God's Word, and submit to the Holy Spirit's leading.

If you are ready to make this decision, please pray with me: *Jesus, I hear You pleading with me to leave my old, sinful lifestyle for a blessed life and eternity with You. Forgive me for ignoring You in the past. I repent of all my sins (please be specific) and I renounce them. By faith, I turn my back on my sinful past to follow You. Please give me the strength to remain under Your loving, protective covering. I am willing to follow You wherever You lead me. Amen.*

CHAPTER 4: DISCUSSION QUESTIONS

1. How can a person know whether his or her dream is from God? What is the ultimate litmus test?

2. How is our relationship with God like that of a bride and bridegroom?

3. How is Laban a type of Satan? Explain why we are considered the devil's children before we come into a relationship with Jesus Christ.

4. Why was it imperative for Jacob, Leah, and Rachel to leave Laban's house? Describe that decision's impact on Israel and us today.

5. What sobering truth does the Holy Spirit reveal through the story of Jacob and Laban? Why is it important for us to take heed to this truth?

6. Consider 2 Corinthians 6:17–18. In what ways is God, like Jacob, calling us to leave our old covering to be in a relationship with Him?

7. How was leaving Laban's home the catalyst to Jacob finding God's version of himself? What lesson can we learn from this?

8. Explain the statement "True love demands a change."

Chapter 5

PARASITISM

In August of 2011, following our beautiful New England wedding, Rochelle and I headed to Florida for our honeymoon. Once there, we took full advantage of the beautiful, sunny weather by planning different outdoor activities each day. One day, while on a riverboat tour, a set of trees stood out to us. At a quick glance, nothing seemed out of the ordinary about them, but after examining them carefully, we realized that there were two different sets of trees appearing to be one set. The main set of tree trunks and branches had branches from another species wrapped around them. The tour guide explained to us what they were. Those trees along the riverbank were the host trees. The other type of trees wrapping itself around the host tree appeared to be the strangler fig, shown in the image at the beginning of this chapter. The strangler fig thrived off the host trees' nutrition yet was gradually killing the host tree in the process.

The host trees and the strangler fig that Rochelle and I saw are an example of parasitism. According to the Merriam-Webster dictionary, parasitism is "an intimate association between organisms of two or more kinds, especially one in which a parasite obtains benefits from a host which it usually injures."[xii] In other words, when you are the host in a parasitic relationship, the guest organism profits at your expense. On our riverboat trip, Rochelle and I couldn't immediately discern the presence of the strangler fig at first glance; we thought we were only looking at one type of tree. Similarly, the danger of a parasitic relationship can be subtle—even undetectable—at times. Let's look at an example of parasitism from Scripture. In Acts 16:16–26 (NIV), Paul and Silas continued their missionary journey, traveling from Troas to Philippi, ancient cities in present-day Greece. In Philippi, they met a slave girl with a unique "gift"—or so it appeared. The author's account of this is as follows:

Once when we were going to the place of prayer, we were met by a female slave who had a spirit by which she predicted the future. She earned a great deal of money for her owners by fortune-telling. She followed Paul and the rest of us, shouting, "These men are servants of the Most High God, who are telling you the way to be saved." She kept this up for many days. Finally Paul became so annoyed that he turned around and said to the spirit, "In the name of Jesus Christ I command you to come out of her!" At that moment the spirit left her. When her owners realized that their hope of making money was gone, they seized Paul and Silas and dragged them into the marketplace to face the authorities. They brought them before the magistrates and said, "These men are Jews, and are throwing our city into an uproar by advocating customs unlawful for us Romans to accept or practice." The crowd joined in the attack against Paul and Silas, and the magistrates ordered them to be stripped and beaten with rods. After they had been severely flogged, they were thrown into prison, and the jailer was commanded to guard them carefully. When he received these orders, he put them in the inner cell and fastened their feet in the stocks. About midnight Paul and Silas were praying and singing hymns to God, and the other prisoners were listening to them. Suddenly there was such a violent earthquake that the foundations of the prison were shaken. At once all the prison doors flew open, and everyone's chains came loose.

Whether or not she realized it, the female slave found herself trapped in a parasitic relationship on two levels. She was under the dominion and exploitation of earthly masters as well as an evil spirit! Being in this situation kept her from locating God's version of herself. It's interesting because, at first glance, one would think that nothing was wrong with the slave girl. Those around her may have marveled at her ability to reveal who Paul and Silas were. Some may have even considered this pious. In fact, wasn't she just affirming that Paul and Silas were men of God who came to point others to salvation through faith in Christ? This is why a parasitic relationship is so dangerous; it can be deceiving to the victim and those around him or her. It can even create a false version of themself as they begin to think that the parasite is a part of who they are. The first example that comes to mind is the LGBTQIA+ community. Their choice to engage in their sinful lifestyle becomes so apparent that it begins to shape their tone, expressions, and mannerism. People refer to them as "flamboyant" or "eccentric," seeing these traits as a part of their personality rather than as the byproduct of Satan's influence and sin. Some of them even claim to be born this way when, in reality, they lost the God-version of themselves.

Please understand that I am not hatefully targeting the LGBTQIA+ community. I think that this is a good moment for me to share my testimony. My parents divorced when I was a baby. I was raised in a single-mother home and saw my father on most weekends. At around four or five years of age, an adult male relative exposed himself to me. I believe that the enemy used that moment to plant a seed in me. Three or four years later when I was eight, I came home from children's church and found a memory verse in my pocket. It was John 3:3 (KJV), where Jesus said to Nicodemus, "Except a man be born again, he cannot see the kingdom of God." In that moment, the Holy Spirit illuminated that verse to me, and I found myself crying out to Jesus, "I want to be born again! I want to see heaven!"

This was the major turning point in my life. Approximately, a year or two later, my mother gave her heart to Christ at an evangelistic crusade. Our shared experience of being born again coupled with the fact that I was the youngest child resulted in a very special bond between me and my mother. My other siblings—ranging from early teens to adult—were not Christians. Favorite TV shows, video games, and our family's artistic side were the extent of what I had in common with my other siblings. We had no spiritual connection, so the depth of fellowship I had was with my mother. We were usually the only ones who attended church on Sundays. We read the Word of God, prayed, and even discussed the spiritual significance of dreams. Looking back, I know that my mother did the best she could to raise us; nevertheless, without a father figure consistently in our home, something was missing. Satan's assignment to manifest the seed of homosexuality planted in my younger years started in junior high school. Unprovoked and with no basis for his claim, another classmate repeatedly hurled gay slurs at me from seventh to eighth grade. Prior to entering ninth grade was when I was first exposed to pornography. I became addicted and eventually found myself attracted to the same sex. Because of my relationship with Christ, I knew that this lifestyle was against the Word of God; I wanted to be free from those desires. Shortly afterward, I informed my mother of my struggle. She would pray with me and affirm who I was in Christ through God's Word. By God's grace, I never physically engaged in homosexuality, but I struggled with my sexual identity for many years. Today I love Jesus, am married to a beautiful woman of God, and have two amazing children. This would not have been possible without my personal relationship with Jesus Christ, God's Word, and the power of the Holy Spirit.

As we read in Acts 16, some parasitic relationships are rooted in a demonic stronghold. Victims of this type of relationship will need to experience deliverance by the power of the Holy Spirit. Another example of this is the demon-possessed boy described in Mark 9:14–29. Jesus's disciples unsuccessfully attempted to cast out the deaf and mute spirit out of the boy; yet, at Jesus's firm command, the spirit left him. When the disciples asked Jesus why they were unable to cast out the spirit, He replied, "This kind can come out by nothing but prayer and fasting" (Mark 9:29, NKJV). We don't earn right standing and favor with God through prayer and fasting; the blood of Jesus Christ alone grants us these. However, fasting and prayer strengthen our spirit man while giving us more power over our fleshly appetites. This is crucial in dealing with a stubborn, persistent demonic stronghold. My spiritual progress against those ungodly desires would not have been possible if I did not allow the Holy Spirit to lead me into seasons of intense prayer and fasting. I believe Paul's authority to cast the evil spirit out of the servant girl was due to his lifestyle of regularly fasting and praying. In 2 Corinthians 11, in describing all the ways he suffered for Christ, Paul included that he often fasted (v. 27). Jesus and Paul needed to fast and pray to see major breakthroughs. This is no different for us; in fact, we should live a regular life in the Spirit through prayer and fasting even after experiencing freedom from bondage. Jesus made it clear that, if we experience deliverance but do not allow His Spirit to fill the vacancy, the evil spirit can return, and the strength of our bondage will be worse than before (Matthew 12:43–45).

We know that, unlike predator/prey relationships which are overtly destructive and apparent in their evil assignment, parasitic relationships can be difficult for one to clearly detect. Sometimes it may even appear that the parasite is there to help, when, in reality, its purpose is to bring harm and ultimately destruction. Take Judas Iscariot, for instance. He was one of Jesus's disciples and even held the position of accountant. On the night of Christ's betrayal, none of the other disciples even suspected that Judas was the traitor. When Jesus told Judas "What you must do, do it quickly," the disciples thought that Jesus sent him to buy more food or to give money to the poor. Like a deadly, subtle parasite, Judas appeared to be helpful, yet was wickedly profiting from Christ and His followers. The Word of God tells us that he stole money from the money bag (John 12:4–6). Eventually, he would betray Christ and cause Him to be crucified for thirty pieces of silver.

In today's world, we hear heartbreaking stories in which some in the elderly community were financially exploited. It is even more tragic when the revealed perpetrators are caregivers, friends, relatives, or even their own children. True to the nature of parasitic relationships, the victims were originally trusting, never suspecting those individuals.

How do we fight against parasitic relationships which prevent us from locating God's version of ourselves? Let's look at some lessons from Paul in Acts 16. Verses 17 and 18 (NIV) tell us, "She followed Paul and the rest of us, shouting, 'These men are servants of the Most High God, who are telling you the way to be saved.' She kept this up for many days. Finally Paul became so annoyed that he turned around and said to the spirit, 'In the name of Jesus Christ I command you to come out of her!' At that moment the spirit left her."

First, we need discernment. As I stated earlier, Paul was a man of God who walked in the Spirit, prayed regularly, and studied the Word of God. This is how he was able to grow in his discernment. He didn't take the servant girl's words at face value because he knew what spirit was behind those words. Furthermore, *when a parasite's ability to profit is threatened, they usually show their true colors.* Consider the actions of the slave girl's owners and Judas Iscariot. After Paul cast the demon out of the girl, her owners became enraged *after realizing that they would no longer profit from her fortune telling.* It was at this point that they reported Paul to the authorities, resulting in Paul's imprisonment. When Mary Magdalene lovingly broke her alabaster box to anoint Jesus's feet, Judas became indignant. He claimed that the expensive box could have been used for the poor, *but the Scripture revealed that his true intention was to take the money for himself.* Shortly after this, Judas consented with the chief priests to betray Christ. Anyone ending a parasitic relationship must prepare themselves for a fight. Remember that God is your greatest ally, and He will lead you to victory if you do not give up!

Second, we need to come to a place in which we are both grieved and angered by parasitic relationships. Another version of these verses (KJV) says that Paul became so grieved that he rebuked that spirit. It is not okay for the enemy to thrive at our expense. A relationship is healthy when it is Christ-centered. Each party involved is edifying the other, helping each other to grow in Christ. One puts the other before themselves—resulting in each having the other's best interests in mind. We need to stop parasitic relationships in their tracks with the authority of Jesus Christ. Just as in a predator/prey relationship, we must keep this key truth in mind: this thing is trying to destroy us! We cannot afford to tolerate it. How would you react if you knew a malaria-filled mosquito landed right on your leg? Would you hesitate or tolerate it for a little while? No! You would immediately crush that thing and run to the doctor right away because malaria is life-threatening. The problem with many of us is that we have become too passive. We're okay with our bondage, even coddling the very thing sent to destroy us. Do you know that even laziness is a parasite that threatens to destroy? Ecclesiastes 4:5 (AMP) tells us, "The fool folds his hands [together] and consumes his own flesh [destroying himself by idleness and apathy]." Bitterness and unforgiveness is a parasite that will destroy its victims if undealt with. Matthew 6:15 (NIV) tells us, "But if you do not forgive others their sins, your Father will not forgive your sins."

The ancient Romans were infamous for their cruel, unusual methods of torture and execution. One method they used was tying a dead corpse to a criminal. Why did they do this? Because they knew that, as the dead person decomposed, the living person would eventually start decomposing simply because they were attached to the dead body. The victim wouldn't die right away; the slow, excruciating process took weeks as the corpse underwent natural decomposition. Many of us fail to grasp the subtle yet deadly association we ended up in. We think we are fine, not realizing that death is slowly yet surely spreading to every area of our lives.

Look at how Jesus cautioned the church of Sardis in Revelation: "I know your deeds; you have a reputation of being alive, but you are dead. Wake up! Strengthen what remains and is about to die, for I have found your deeds unfinished in the sight of my God" (Revelation 3:1–2, NIV). Notice that Jesus did not tell the Sardinians to resuscitate what was dead; He encouraged them to strengthen the things which remained. In other words, nurture those things and individuals conducive to your spiritual growth and physical well-being. Do not waste your time and energy associating with toxic things or individuals who have no intention of turning to Christ. Cut them off! Like the victim tied to a dead corpse, staying connected to them will ultimately result in your death. Some things in our lives will never be good for us, so why waste time trying to make them good? Some of you are dying spiritually because you are staying connected to someone who is happy to remain spiritually dead. It's time for you to let them go!

I am not saying that this is an easy decision. We read what Paul and Christ experienced when they dealt with the parasites in their lives. Paul was beaten, arrested, and imprisoned. Eventually he would die by beheading under Emperor Nero in Rome. Jesus Christ was betrayed, arrested, beaten, and crucified. Depending on your situation, it could cost you your comfort, livelihood, opportunities, or other resources. You could end up in a legal battle. For others, it could cost you relationships. In more severe cases, like Christ and Paul, it could cost you your freedom—or, possibly, even your very life. If you don't remember anything else that I have said, please remember this: the cost of being Christ's disciple is at the very core of finding our God-version. "Then Jesus said to His disciples, 'If anyone desires to come after Me, let him deny himself, and take up his cross, and follow Me. For whoever desires to save his life will lose it, but whoever loses his life for My sake will find it. For what profit is it to a man if he gains the whole world, and loses his own soul? Or what will a man give in exchange for his soul?'" (Matthew 16:24–26, NKJV). If you are connected to anything or anyone toxic, please ask yourself, "Is it worth God's plan for my life? Is it worth my very soul?"

In Mark 10:17–31, Jesus met a man entangled in another type of parasitic relationship. According to the Scripture, this wealthy young man was initially eager for eternal life, even requesting for Christ to show him how to acquire it. Christ knew his heart well, listing different commandments that the young man attested to having followed since he was a youth. However, Christ knew that there was one thing that kept the young man from following Him. You see, at some point, all of us will have to confront that one thing which threatens to keep us from locating the God-version of ourselves. Jesus said to him, "One thing you lack…. Go, sell everything you have and give to the poor, and you will have treasure in heaven. Then come, follow me" (v. 21, NIV). The rich young man's response was very unfortunate: He walked away, sorrowful, because he was unwilling to let go of the wealth he amassed. It is not a sin to be wealthy; however, the problem was that he could not let go of his wealth to follow Christ. The man had a parasitic relationship with greed.

It's interesting that we do not know the name of this rich young man. Had he listened to Christ, sold everything he had, and followed Him, we may have heard this man's name mentioned along with Peter, James, John, and other godly people in the New Testament. His parasitic relationship with greed robbed him of his spiritual identity and legacy that could have lasted to this very day. I'm truly convinced that many of us do not understand the magnitude of what we are forfeiting when we allow spiritual parasites to remain in our lives. Let's go back to what I said earlier: What is that one thing in your life preventing you from relocating God's version of yourself?

Please pray with me: *Holy Spirit, thank You for guiding me to the truth. I pray that You would expose any parasites in my life preventing me from following Christ wholeheartedly and give me the power to get rid of them. In Jesus's name I pray, amen.*

CHAPTER 5: DISCUSSION QUESTIONS

1. How can a parasitic relationship be subtle or undetectable? Consider Acts 16:16–26.

2. Why is consistency in prayer and God's Word crucial to detecting parasites in our lives?

3. Describe how a parasitic relationship can appear helpful.

4. When does a parasite usually show its true colors?

5. Why should we be both grieved and angered by parasitic relationships?

6. How does the Roman method of tying a dead corpse to a criminal relate to parasitic relationships? What does this mean for us today?

7. What is at the very core of finding God's version of ourselves?

8. Take a moment and silently consider: What is that one thing that may be keeping you from following Christ wholeheartedly? Now, after you identify that thing, surrender it to Christ and ask Him to lead you to someone (pastor, trustworthy friend, spouse, etc.) who will help you deal with it.

Chapter 6

MUTUALISM

So far, each biological relationship previously discussed has had negative spiritual implications. This final relationship that we will discuss ends on a brighter note! As its name suggests, mutualism is an association that equally benefits organisms of two different species.[xiii] The bee and flower in the image are mutually benefiting from each other. The bee needs pollen from the flower in order to survive; the flower continues to produce offspring through cross-pollination as the bee travels to other flowers. Mutualistic arrangements are most likely to develop between organisms with widely different living requirements. This definition reminds me how different we are from God. In Isaiah 55:8–9 (NKJV), God says, "'For My thoughts are not your thoughts, nor are your ways My ways,' says the LORD. 'For as the heavens are higher than the earth, so are My ways higher than your ways, and My thoughts than your thoughts.'" Yet, despite how different we are from Him and how undeserving we are of His goodness, He willingly shows us kindness. Psalm 8:3–4 (NIV) says, "When I consider your heavens, the work of your fingers, the moon and the stars, which you have set in place, what is mankind that you are mindful of them, human beings that you care for them?" One of the mind-blowing ways God demonstrates kindness is by granting us the unmerited privilege of partnering with Him.

The Word of God tells us that He has called us to mutually partner with Him in three specific ways. First, we are called to mutually partner with God in fellowship that starts with a relationship with Him. We see a clear example of this in Revelation 3:14–22 when Christ addressed the Laodicean church. He told them, "Those whom I love I rebuke and discipline. So be earnest and repent. Here I am! I stand at the door and knock. If anyone hears my voice and opens the door, I will come in and eat with that person, and they with me (Revelation 3:19–20, NIV)."

Mutualism is more than just inviting Jesus Christ into one's heart as the initial act of faith. Meals in the biblical Jewish culture served to reconcile enemies, establish unity, and deepen friendships. There's something key about how Christ said He would eat with us. "I will ... eat with that person, and they with me." Let me paint a picture for you: You and a really good friend decide to spend time together at your house. Your entire day was spent putting effort and care into preparing a delicious meal for them. Likewise, your friend was excited to come to your house for dinner, and they also brought their signature dish with them. You know it's going to be good. You both take the time to sit at the beautifully spread table. You eat from her dish; she eats from yours. You laugh at times, cry at times, share wonderful memories, and discuss plans for the future. At times, you both just sit in thoughtful silence, and because you know your friend so well, you communicate with her without saying a word. This is how Christ wants to fellowship with us. Yes, salvation is wonderful, and there is nothing wrong with regular church attendance. However, there is so much more to enjoying a mutualistic relationship with Christ! In my illustration, the eating of each other's food represents a mutualistic relationship in which each party fully appreciates and engages in the feelings, words, and interests of the other. This is what Christ desires in His relationship with you. He wants to bless you and He wants to be blessed by you. You may ask, "How can I bless God?" We bless Him in many ways, such as through our worship, obedience, spending time with Him, and by sharing His love with others. All these things are food to His soul. On the flip side, imagine going to a friend's house and both of you have meals to share with each other. Wouldn't it be strange if your friend wanted you to eat his food, but he was unwilling to eat your food? What thoughts would run through your mind? "Does he think I'm a bad cook?" "Why isn't he considerate of the fact that I took the time to prepare this meal for him?" "Does he even care that I took the time to prepare a meal for him?" This is how Christ feels when we go into His presence but make the conversation all about us—our needs, our dreams, our plans—with no consideration of what He desires for us. Or perhaps we went to our friend's house without bringing anything and we wanted to eat all their food (none of us has ever done that before, right??). This is a type of relationship with Christ in which a person wants to enjoy all the benefits that Christ has to offer them—salvation, blessings, promotion, favor, to name a few. However, there is no interest in bringing one's life, heart, time, talent, or treasures for Christ to use for His purposes. This is the unfortunate reality for many who claim to be in a relationship with Christ. Remember, in a mutualistic relationship, each party brings something to the table that benefits the other.

Second, we are called to mutually partner with God through fellowshipping with Him in His sufferings. In Philippians 3:10 (NKJV), Paul the apostle expresses this desire: "that I may know Him and the power of His resurrection, and the fellowship of His sufferings, being conformed to His death." He also states in 2 Timothy 2:12 (KJV), "If we suffer, we shall also reign with him: if we deny him, he also will deny us." Suffering with Christ is the least desirable part of mutualism to our carnal man—yet it is impossible to truly walk in a mutualistic relationship with Christ without suffering with Him. I want you to think about your closest, deepest, intimate human relationship. Take a moment and consider this: What brings depth to your relationship with that other person? Was it being able to enjoy good times and lighthearted moments together? Was it when both of you were winning and on top, so to speak? Or did you both experience some type of adversity that tested and even strengthened your relationship? I think about my relationship with my wife Rochelle. We had some moments of joy and revelry in our early years. When we were younger and in college, we would go on fun trips with friends, enjoy amusement parks together, watch movies, walk through Broadway in New York City—and there was nothing wrong with those moments. We also went through very challenging times and, yes, we had our intense moments of conflict and disagreement. However, it was in those tough moments that our relationship and love for each other deepened. I can truly call Rochelle my best friend because we know everything about each other—good, bad, and ugly—yet we love and are committed to each other. This is what God wants with you. He wants to challenge your faith and devotion to Him so that it can become stronger. Our profession of love to Him are mere words if they are not tested by the storms of life. He desires to take you deeper into fellowship with Him—but this will require your willingness to suffer with Him.

Finally, we are called to mutually partner with God through co-reigning with Him. Second Timothy 2:12 tells us that if we suffer with Him, we will also reign with Him. Romans 8:17 (NIV) says, "Now if we are children, then we are heirs—heirs of God and co-heirs with Christ, if indeed we share in his sufferings in order that we may also share in his glory." In Revelation 3:21 (NIV), Christ promises, "To the one who is victorious, I will give the right to sit with me on my throne, just as I was victorious and sat down with my Father on his throne." These Scriptures share the fact that co-reigning with Christ accompanies one suffering with Christ. It is both comforting and encouraging to know that, when we endure adversity and hardship for the sake of our relationship with Christ, the outcome will be glorious for us—both in this life and in the life to come!

First, let's look at this life. Christ promised those who believed in Him—from His disciples in ancient Israel all the way to us in the twenty-first century—would accomplish greater things than He did on this earth. In John 14:12 (NIV), He said, "Very truly I tell you, whoever believes in me will do the works I have been doing, and they will do even greater things than these, because I am going to the Father." Why was Jesus's going to the Father so crucial? Because after Jesus Christ rose from the dead, He had to ascend to the right hand of God the Father first before Holy Spirit could descend upon believers. It is crucial for all believers to be filled with and empowered by Holy Spirit because He is the One who gives us the power to do the greater works Christ spoke of. Think about it: Christ did tremendous things on earth such as heal lepers, give the blind sight, feed multitudes, and raise the dead. He is saying that we have the power to do this and more! These are some of the benefits of co-reigning with Christ on this earth. We will also operate in this authority in the life to come—starting at the commencement of the 1,000-year reign of Christ with His followers on earth. In Revelation 20:4–6 (NIV), John the apostle testified:

> *I saw thrones on which were seated those who had been given authority to judge. And I saw the souls of those who had been beheaded because of their testimony about Jesus and because of the word of God. They had not worshipped the beast or its image and had not received its mark on their foreheads or their hands. They came to life and reigned with Christ a thousand years. (The rest of the dead did not come to life until the thousand years were ended.) This is the first resurrection. Blessed and holy are those who share in the first resurrection. The second death has no power over them, but they will be priests of God and of Christ and will reign with him for a thousand years.*

Following a time on earth called the great tribulation (see Daniel 9:27, 12:11–12; Matthew 24:15–16), Christ will return in physical form to reign over the whole earth from His capital, Jerusalem. Christ confirmed this when He said to His disciples, "Truly I tell you, at the renewal of all things, when the Son of Man sits on his glorious throne, you who have followed me will also sit on twelve thrones, judging the twelve tribes of Israel. And everyone who has left houses or brothers or sisters or father or mother or wife or children or fields for my sake will receive a hundred times as much and will inherit eternal life" (Matthew 19:28–29, NIV). Both portions of Scripture reveal that those blessed with the privilege of co-reigning with Christ first experienced a time of suffering or loss for His sake. During Christ's temptation in the wilderness, Satan wanted to offer Christ a cheap imitation of victory—one that did not require the suffering that accompanies obedience to God. Thankfully, Christ never succumbed to the devil's schemes. On the contrary, He was our perfect example. He resisted the temptation to claim the throne without the cross. He showed us how to suffer patiently, receiving God's blessings in His way and timing. When we submit to God's will for our lives and endure suffering for His sake, we can be certain that we will also reign with Him!

One important thing for us to understand is that we are not just partners with God—we are a part of God Himself! Yes, we know that God is Spirit; mankind is flesh and blood. However, as I mentioned in the introduction, we were made in God's image—which, in the original language, means that we were cut out from Him. We literally have God's DNA in us!

A few months before writing this book, a couple invited me over to their house for a prayer meeting. A brother in Christ at the meeting shared some fascinating information about the DNA sequencing in the human body. I did further research on the website Erev Shabbat. Here's what I found. The DNA double helix is formed when a certain number of acids in a row forms a bridge. A bridge is formed after every 10th, 5th, 6th, and 5th acid. This pattern is continuous.

When Jewish scientists heard about this discovery, they were amazed. Why? In the Hebrew language, there are no specific characters for numbers. Hebrew letters and their combinations represent each number. If you look at the Hebrew letters corresponding to the sequence, the letters form YHWH, God's name![xiv] This amazing discovery further confirms that our true, authentic selves originated from God Himself—not the world, and certainly not Satan. Therefore, it is incumbent on us to seek Him to understand who we are and where we fit in His overall plan.

We relocate Christ's version of ourselves when we are willing to admit that we may have lost our way. God's question to Adam and Eve after they sinned, "Where art thou?" challenges us to really examine ourselves and to confront the fact that we may be far away from the person God originally intended for us to be. Relocating God's version of ourselves also requires our willingness to reevaluate the types of relationships we are in, determining if they are pushing us closer to God or leading us further away from Him. We must be willing to detach from those places, habits, ideologies, and even individuals who threaten to destroy the person God originally intended us to be. Above all, we must be willing to go deeper in relationship with the One who created us in His image, loves us beyond what we can imagine, and who always has our best interest in mind.

Let's pray: *Jesus, thank You for the opportunity to have a personal, mutualistic relationship with You. I acknowledge that it cost You Your very life on the cross for this to happen. With heartfelt gratitude, I surrender all that I am to know You and find my true identity in You alone. Amen.*

CHAPTER 6: DISCUSSION QUESTIONS

1. In what ways is a mutualistic relationship with God unique and mind-blowing?

2. How were ancient Jewish meals symbolic of the type of relationship Christ wants to establish with us?

3. Why is it important for a mutualistic relationship with God to be reciprocal (equal effort on both sides)?

4. Why is enduring suffering important in a mutualistic relationship with Christ?

5. Describe the benefits of mutual partnership with God in this present life and in the age to come.

6. Rather than only being partners with God, how are we a part of God Himself?

7. How does science confirm that mankind was truly made in God's image?

8. Now that you have read this book, what steps are you willing to take in order to relocate God's version of you?

Chapter 7

WHY THIS MATTERS

BRRRIIIIIIIIIIIIIIIIIING!!!

The shrill, piercing bell marked the beginning of last period. My high school alma mater rested in a section of Denver favorable for sightseers. Ninety-four miles southwest of the school, Pikes Peak displayed snowcaps mingled with majestic greenery. Wyoming's border was 107 miles north—a favorite for Coloradans who wanted to purchase fireworks legally.

It was my senior world literature class. The passion I fostered for writing and storytelling followed me up from my elementary years, so naturally, this was my favorite subject. Mr. B's passion for this subject—coupled with his cool, friendly, and welcoming persona—further magnified my enjoyment of this class.

I fidgeted nervously in my chair as Mr. B grabbed the huge stack of papers from his desk. It was the graded narrative assignment in which we had to write our own spin-off from the classic poem "Dante's Inferno" the first of three poems in the "Divine Comedy," written by the fourteenth century author, Dante Alighieri.

My heart rate accelerated as he dropped my paper on my desk. I hesitated for a moment before looking down at the graded paper.

Well, here goes, I prepped myself.

I glanced down at the paper. An A! I breathed a huge sigh of relief. I knew that I had poured so much time, detail, and craft into the assignment. It was reassuring to know that my efforts hadn't been in vain.

Mr. B's world lit class was one of a few key monumental life experiences that helped shape me into the person that I am today. You see, not only did Mr. B recognize and cultivate the gift I possessed; he went a step further. He recommended me to a national organization that recruited and paired up recent high school graduates with teachers in helping at-risk middle school students successfully complete summer school. Wisely, I accepted the opportunity and quickly fell in love with the world of secondary education. Years later, I completed my undergraduate and graduate studies, becoming a state-licensed educator. As I write this book, I have entered my fifteenth year of teaching.

I tell this story to emphasize the depth of influence a teacher has on his or her students. According to the National Association of Elementary School Principals (NAESP), young people between the ages of five and eighteen spend approximately 13 percent of their time at school.[xv] If we focus only on weekdays, the percentage increases to 25 percent—one-fourth of the child's day. This is enough time to affect the shaping of students' ideologies, values, self-perception, and (as was my case) future aspirations. A teacher's influence during this limited time can be far reaching, inspiring students to become world changers in every career sector—but, most importantly, the best version of themselves God created them to be.

The results can also be catastrophic. God gave me the unique opportunity to spend a significant portion of my life on both sides of the teacher's desk, so I am well equipped to say that public education today is drastically different from twenty-five years ago when I was a high school senior. However, the quickly spreading inferno started as little embers when I was still a kid. One of Satan's major schemes started brewing around the 1980s. Members of the gay, lesbian, and bisexual community emulated Black Americans' fight for equal rights and social justice in the 1960's Civil Rights Movement. Under the assertion of their lifestyle's link to genetics—scientifically unproven—the gay and lesbian community pushed for rights such as homosexual marriage, gays in the military, and other legislation-based changes that would morph the social, political, occupational, and spiritual landscape of our country and world.[xvi] I must digress for a moment to state that, as a United States citizen, I believe in "liberty and justice for all," as stated in our Pledge of Allegiance. However, true patriotism will adhere to the entire pledge, including the words "one nation under God." For us to be truly one nation under God means that we submit ourselves to His Word—even those parts of His Word which challenge our current lifestyles.

Then in the late 1980s, a curriculum called "The Children of the Rainbow" was introduced to New York City public schools, sparking mass controversy at the time. New York Mayor David Dinkins adhered to calls from gay and lesbian organizations to expose students to their lifestyles to promote tolerance and acceptance. Many parents and educators questioned the curriculum's role in forming students' morality. They also questioned the appropriateness of its contents such as books within the curriculum titled *Heather Has Two Mommies* and *Daddy's Roommate*. At the time, more than half of New York City's school boards—consisting of parents, teachers, and administrators—rejected all or part of the curriculum. Regardless of how strong the opposition, then Chancellor Joseph A. Fernandez's ultimatum for the schools—"follow the Rainbow Curriculum or come up with your own that addresses same-sex families"—prevailed.[xvii]

Initially framed as an effort to promote awareness and tolerance, the LGBTQIA+ agenda has reached an unprecedented level of aggressiveness in public schools today. In grades as early as kindergarten, students deemed unsure of their sexuality are provided education, options, and support by school-based staff in their exploration of changing genders—with no regard to their family values or parental consent. Many of the occurrences I will mention took place in educational settings that I previously worked in. To avoid accusations of libel, I withheld the names of people and locations, at times providing fictitious names for clarity of writing.

In one school district, a couple were outraged after attending a meeting at their daughter's school.

"Why are you calling our daughter Justin when we named her Sarah?!" they demanded of teachers and administrators. "She is female!"

Another instance took place when I attended a district-wide diversity, equity, and inclusion (DEI) taskforce meeting. Members on the committee bemoaned the potential backlash they might receive from some parents regarding a book they were planning to include in the kindergarten curriculum. The fictional "children's" book centered on a character who received a magic wand which gave them the power to change themselves from male to female and back. Later in the book, the child acquired the power to remain in the gender of their choice. As they continued to speak disapprovingly of parental objectors, the Holy Spirit prompted me to speak.

"A DEI taskforce is branded as such with the expectation that the background of all students, parents, and educators are taken into consideration, correct?"

"Yes," the members all agreed.

"Well," I continued, "if this taskforce prides itself on being inclusive, shouldn't it also consider the viewpoints and convictions of more conservative families whose morals and beliefs do not align with books such as these?"

No one responded to my argument; all I received were blank stares. Then another member changed the subject, and the meeting continued.

I was, once again, reminded of some bleak realities. First, the LGBTQIA+ agenda has no interest in allowing respectful disagreement on their values and endeavors within education today. Secondly, Satan is using their role in the schools to impose perverse ideologies robbing the younger generation of their God-given identity while they are still impressionable. It is a shame that educated adults would even consent to a child's decision to change genders when he or she is too young to understand the implications of their choice. We know from science that the frontal lobe—the part of the brain responsible for decision-making—does not start developing until a child's adolescent years and is fully developed around a person's mid-twenties. Kids do not fully grasp the fact that the decision to change genders will alter their bodies and result in long-term effects which are, in some cases, irreversible. The psychological toll this takes on transgender youth is also apparent. According to a 2022 news article from the publication *Medical News Today*, transgender teens are 7.6 times more likely to attempt suicide when compared to heterosexual, cisgender peers.[xviii] Let's call this what it is: child abuse.

Please understand: this book is not an attack on public education; however, I am addressing public education to expose major ways in which Satan is attempting to rob us and future generations of our God-given identity. From district offices to individual classrooms, there are decisions being made concerning students' education that parents should know yet don't know. The sad truth is that many of these decisions are stripping parents of their right to raise their children based on the values they have established within their homes. It is as if the state is entering in your home and declaring to you, "We are now the decision-maker for your children as it relates to beliefs, ideology, and—yes—even sexuality." No, it's even worse than this example because it is happening covertly. Parents cannot confront what they are unaware of. Second Corinthians 2:11 tells us that we are not to be ignorant of Satan's devices.

Each generation becomes increasingly more wicked than the previous one due to either passivity, ignorance, or both. In Hosea 4:6 (NIV), God states, "My people are destroyed from lack of knowledge." The downward trend of Christianity in America echoes this sentiment. According to Pew Research, the percentage of Americans professing to be Christian has significantly declined. In the late 1970s, 90 percent of Americans called themselves Christian verses 65 percent in 2019.[xix] According to Pew Charitable Trusts, "Center's projections show Christians shrinking from 64% of Americans of all ages in 2020 to between 54% and 35% by 2070."[xx] We will continue to exacerbate the problem if we do not prayerfully, lovingly, yet firmly confront Satan's efforts to rob America and other nations of their God-given identity.

The purpose of this book is threefold. First, I pray that you would recognize and avoid the counterfeit identities originating from the world and Satan. After the Holy Spirit brings you awareness, my next prayer for you is that you would discover and embrace your biblical, God-given identity. Finally understanding who God intended for you to be, I pray that you would lovingly yet truthfully help others on their journey of discovering the best possible version of themselves—God's version.

CHAPTER 7: DISCUSSION QUESTIONS

1. Describe the positive ways in which education can have an impact on a child's identity.

2. How did Satan infiltrate the Civil Rights Movement? What was the impact on American society?

3. What does it mean to be "one nation under God"?

4. In what ways are family values being challenged within public schools? What potential threat does this pose to the identity of future generations?

5. What is true inclusion? Give details.

6. Why is it preposterous—and even damaging—to allow children to determine their sexual identity?

7. In Hosea 4:6 (NIV), God states, "My people are destroyed from lack of knowledge." How is this playing out in our society today?

8. What measures will it take for us to see our society return to its God-given identity? Prayerfully commit to understanding and fulfilling your role in making this happen.

ENDNOTES

i. "A BRIEF HISTORY OF GPS." Aerospace. Accessed March 11, 2024 <https://authorsequity.org>

ii. "Global Positioning System History." Jermaine Walker. Published October 27, 2012 <https://www.nasa.gov/general/global-positioning-system-history/#:~:text=Embracing%20previous%20ideas%20from%20Navy,became%20fully%20operational%20in%201993>

iii. "6754. tselem." Bible Hub. Accessed March 11, 2024 <https://biblehub.com/hebrew/6754.htm>

iv. "1823. demuth." Bible Hub. Accessed March 11, 2024 <https://biblehub.com/hebrew/1823.htm>

v. "7287. radah." Bible Hub. Accessed March 11, 2024 <https://biblehub.com/hebrew/7287.htm>

vi. "Five Types of Ecological Relationships." David H. Nguyen. Accessed March 11, 2024 <https://education.seattlepi.com/predation-biology-3352.html>

vii. "Advertising spending in North America from 2000 to 2024." J.G. Navarro. Statista. Published September 19, 2023 <https://www.statista.com/statistics/429036/advertising-expenditure-in-north-america/#:~:text=It%20was%20calculated%20that%20the,the%20impact%20of%20the%20coronavirus>

viii. "Lexicon :: Strong's G2380 – *thyō*." Blue Letter Bible. Accessed March 11, 2024 <https://www.blueletterbible.org/lexicon/g2380/kjv/tr/0-1/>

ix. "622. apollumi." Bible Hub. Accessed March 11, 2024 <https://biblehub.com/greek/622.htm>

x. "Interspecific competition." Last updated on June 16, 2022 <https://www.biologyonline.com/dictionary/interspecific-competition>

xi. "Commensalism." BiologyOnline. Updated February 9, 2022 <https://www.biologyonline.com/dictionary/commensalism>

xii. Ibid.

xiii. "Lexicon :: Strong's G3340 – *metanoeō*." Blue Letter Bible. Accessed March 11, 2024 <https://www.blueletterbible.org/lexicon/g3340/kjv/tr/0-1/>

xiv. "Parasitism." Merriam-Webster. Accessed February 21, 2024 <https://www.merriam-webster.com/dictionary/parasitism>

xv. "Mutualism." BiologyOnline. Last updated July 21, 2021 <https://www.biologyonline.com/dictionary/mutualism>

xvi. "YHWH is genetically coded into us." Sipos Richard. Published January 3, 2023 <https://erevshabbat.org/en/yhwh-is-genetically-coded-into-us/>

xvii. "Ensuring student success requires group effort." Bruce Congleton. Published October 24, 2021 <https://lasvegassun.com/news/2021/oct/24/ensuring-student-success-requires-group-effort/>

xviii. "Queering the Schools." Marjorie King. 2003. *City Journal* <https://www.city-journal.org/article/queering-the-schools >

xix. "Under 'Rainbow,' a War: When Politics, Morals and Learning Mix." Josh Barbanel. *New York Times*: December 27, 1992 <https://www.nytimes.com/1992/12/27/nyregion/under-rainbow-a-war-when-politics-morals-and-learning-mix.html>

xx. "Transgender teens 7.6 times more likely to attempt suicide." Corrie Pelc. Medical News Today. Published June 14, 2022 <https://www.medicalnewstoday.com/articles/transgender-teens-7-6-times-more-likely-to-attempt-suicide>

xxi. "What Is the Future of Religion in America?" David O'Reilly. The Pew Charitable Trusts. Published February 7, 2023 <https://www.pewtrusts.org/en/trust/archive/winter-2023/what-is-the-future-of-religion-in-america>

PHOTO SOURCES

Chapter 1 Photo Source: https://www.nccg.org/lion_chasing_deer.jpg

Chapter 2 Photo Source: https://www.pinterest.com/pin/841539880404282609/

Chapter 3 Photo Source: https://www.flickr.com/photos/francesco_veronesi/

Chapter 4 Photo Source: https://www.flickr.com/photos/westoshafloral/3939014412/

Chapter 5 Photo Source: https://www.mapquest.com/travel/dangerous-animals.htm

Chapter 6 Photo Source: https://www.backyard-beekeepers.org/

Chapter 7 Photo Source: https://www.lightstock.com/photos/crowd-of-teenagers-on-street

Printed in the USA
CPSIA information can be obtained
at www.ICGtesting.com
JSHW011621290724
67153JS00001B/6